Astronauts

Written by Julie Connal ◉ Illustrated by Marjorie Scott

People who fly into space
are called astronauts.
Astronauts are men and women
who are usually scientists and pilots.

Before they fly into space,
astronauts learn about living in space.

They must spend time learning about their spacecraft and how it works.

They will spend time
getting used to the spacesuits
they must wear.

They must spend time learning how to get used to *weightlessness*, or the lack of *gravity*, in space.

Each space flight is called a *mission*.
During each mission,
astronauts gather information.

They take photographs,
and they send television pictures
of space and planets back to Earth.

When astronauts landed on the moon,
some of them traveled around
in a four-wheeled *lunar rover*.
They collected many samples
of rocks and dust.

Astronauts also repair things.
On one special mission,
astronauts flew into space
in a space shuttle
to fix a large telescope
that *orbits* the Earth.

We still have much to learn
about space.
On space missions,
astronauts help us find out
a little more information each time.

Glossary

gravity—pull or force that attracts objects to the center of the earth.

lunar rover—a four-wheeled space vehicle.

mission—trip that has a purpose, or tasks that must be carried out.

orbit—path or course around the planet Earth.

weightlessness—a lightness, caused by lack of gravity in space.